PIECEWORK MAGAZINE PRESENTS

THE

NEEDLEWORKER'S
COMPANION

SHAY PENDRAY

D0967483

INTERWEAVE PRESS
www.interweave.com

The Needleworker's Companion by Shay Pendray

Editor: Jeane Hutchins
Copy editor: Stephen Beal
Proofreader: Nancy Arndt

Illustrator: Marjorie Leggitt
Book design and production: Dean Howes

Text copyright © 2002, Shay Pendray
Illustrations copyright © 2002, Marjorie Leggitt
Interweave Press

201 East Fourth Street
Loveland, Colorado 80537
USA
www.interweave.com

Printed and bound in China through Asia Pacific Offset

Library of Congress Cataloging-in-Publication Data

Pendray, Shay.
  Needleworker's companion / Shay Pendray.
        p. cm.
Includes index.
  ISBN 1-931499-07-1
  1. Needlework. I. Title.
  TT750 .P42 2002
  746.4--dc21

                                    2002000054

10 9 8 7 6 5 4 3 2

Preface

In the past twenty-five years, I have taught thousands of needlework students, beginners to advanced, in my store and in guilds across the nation. The answers to the questions that students ask, and the kind of knowledge they seek, are covered in this handy compendium of needlework techniques.

How do you thread a needle? How do you end a thread? What kind of needle should you use? What size? For beginners, and for those who seek a refresher, this book covers the basics. Use it to remind yourself how to start stitching with an away waste knot or look up how many strands of floss are needed to cover 14-count canvas.

This little book also provides generous instruction in advanced techniques, including how and when to use the very valuable sinking thread. Here, among many other subjects, you'll learn how to block, mount, and clean your projects. And there's a nice long chapter on the stitches themselves, complete with detailed, step-by-step instructions.

This companion is for all needleworkers who want to improve their technique. Embroidery takes dedication, concentration, and practice, practice, practice. First, you learn the concepts with your mind, and then practice teaches your fingers to stitch with perfection.

Happy Stitching,

Shay Pendray

Shay Pendray

CONTENTS

TYPES OF NEEDLEWORK 6

Counted Cross-Stitch 6
Needlepoint 7
Blackwork 7
Bargello 8
Stumpwork 8
Drawn Thread Work 8
Pulled Thread
Embroidery 8
Crewelwork 9
Bead Embroidery 9
Ribbon Embroidery 9
Hardanger 9

FABRICS 10

Canvas 10
Mono Canvas 11

Interlocking Canvas 12
Duo Canvas 12
Waste Canvas 13
Plastic Canvas 13
Congress Cloth 13
Silk Gauze 14
Aida Fabric 14
Evenweave Linen 15
Care and Storage 16

THREADS 17

Stitchable 17
Wool 17
Tapestry Yarn 19
Crewel Wool 19
Cotton 20
Perle Cotton 20
Silk 23
Linen 24
Nonstitchable 27
Coverage 28

Color 31

NEEDLES 33

Tapestry 33
Chenille 35
Couching 35
Holding 35
Embroidery/Crewel 7
Care 37
Darners 37
Needle Threader 38

TOOLS 39

Scissors 39
Lights and Lamps 40
Laying Tools 40

TRANSFERRING A DESIGN 43

To Canvas 43
To Fabric 44

MOUNTING FABRIC 45

Roller Frame 45
Stretcher Bars 49
Embroidery Hoops 50

STARTING A THREAD 53

Waste Knot 53
Pinhead Stitch 54
Away Waste Knot 55
"L" Stitch 56
½-Thread Method 57
Knot on the Back 57
Couching Thread 58

ENDING A THREAD 59

Weaving In 59
Waste Ending 60
Pinhead Stitches 61
"L" Stitch 62

Whipping Down 62

SINKING NEEDLE 63

STARTING TO STITCH 66

Thread Length 66
Threading the Needle . . .66
Where to Start 67

THE STITCHES 68

Tent 68
Cross-Stitch 68
Diagonal Tent
(Basketweave) 69
Half-Cross 69
Continental 69
Outline 75
Couching and Outline . . .76
Stitch Diagrams 79

Stitches for Small Areas .80
Textured Stitches 84
Stitches for Stems,
Narrow Lines, Outlines . .88
Stitches for Backgrounds,
Large Areas 91
Miscellaneous Stitches . .97
Compensating the
Stitches 100

FIXING MISTAKES 102

**BLOCKING, FRAMING,
FINISHING** 104

**CLEANING
NEEDLEWORK** 107

RESOURCES 108

INDEX 110

TYPES OF NEEDLEWORK

Needlework is the decoration of cloth with a needle and thread. This all-encompassing term covers counted thread, such as needlepoint and cross-stitch, and surface embroidery techniques (embellishing an uncounted ground with stitches to form patterns and/or pictures or decorate clothing). Most types share the same stitches. There are a number of techniques and some are known by several different names.

Counted Cross-Stitch is worked on an unmarked, *evenweave ground* fabric by following a chart. Each chart square represents a single cross-stitch on the fabric. On dual fabrics, the stitch is from hole to hole; on single-weave fabrics, the stitch is usually worked over two threads. Each chart square has a symbol that represents a color of thread.

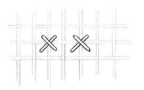

**Cross-stitch on
single-weave fabric**

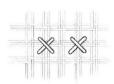

**Cross-stitch on
dual fabric**

Needlepoint is the common name for the *counted technique* of covering a canvas ground with counted stitches; it is also known as **canvas work**.

Blackwork is worked on a *counted ground* fabric using stitches to form repeat patterns. Patterns range from simple to complex and are usually worked in black thread. Blackwork may be stitched so the front and back of the stitching look the same using the double running stitch, which is always worked in two journeys.

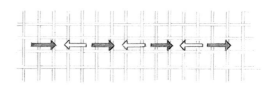

Two journeys of a double running stitch—black first, white second.

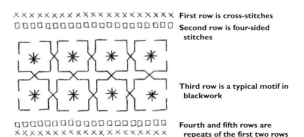

First row is cross-stitches

Second row is four-sided stitches

Third row is a typical motif in blackwork

Fourth and fifth rows are repeats of the first two rows

Blackwork motif

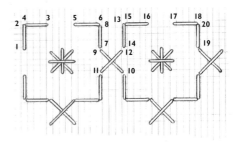

Stitch diagram for Blackwork motif

Bargello, also called Hungarian point, Florentine embroidery, and flame stitch, is worked on a *counted ground* fabric, usually in wool or silk in continuous upright stitches in repeated sequences of color and pattern.

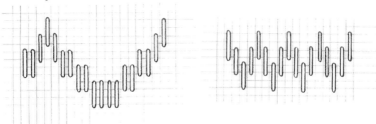

Typical Bargello patterns

Stumpwork, also referred to as raised work, padded work, embossed work, or dimensional work, is characterized by padding and raising stitched areas to achieve a *dimensional effect*.

Drawn Thread Work is stitched on an *evenweave ground* fabric, usually linen; the threads of the ground fabric are drawn or extracted out of the fabric to leave actual holes. The remaining threads are decorated with needle-weaving techniques or worked over with stitches.

Pulled Thread Embroidery is a *counted-thread* technique often stitched on white ground fabric with white thread (one type of *whitework*). The threads of the ground fabric are compressed by pulling stitches tightly; the tighter the stitch is pulled, the larger the opening in the fabric. Threads are never extracted from the ground fabric.

Crewelwork utilizes traditional embroidery stitches but it is done with a two-ply crewel wool thread on an *uncounted linen* ground fabric, preferably twill.

Bead Embroidery is worked with a half–cross stitch over two threads on canvas and with a tent stitch for all other fabrics. Small seed beads are *sewn* on to a ground fabric one at a time.

Ribbon Embroidery is often used to depict realistic flowers. Silk or satin *ribbon* is applied to a ground fabric with embroidery or ribbon embroidery stitches.

Hardanger is stitched on an *evenweave ground* fabric, traditionally 22 count (another type of *whitework*). A series of kloster blocks, usually a set of five satin stitches over four threads, are stitched in preparation for cutting and removing threads, and for decorating the remaining threads with needle-weaving techniques.

Dashes indicate cut lines

Pinhead stitch

Kloster blocks

Needleweaving

FABRICS

Termed **ground** or ground fabric, a wide variety of fabrics are suitable, including canvas, silk, wool, cotton, and linen. *All counted thread work is stitched on evenweave fabrics. Nonevenweave fabrics are suitable for all types of surface embroidery.*

An evenweave fabric has equally spaced horizontal and vertical threads of the same thickness. The number of threads per running inch determines the gauge or **count** of an evenweave fabric. The higher the number, the finer the fabric; e.g., 18-count is finer than 14-count.

DETERMINING THE COUNT OF EVENWEAVE FABRIC

Place a ruler along a horizontal thread. Line up an inch marker with a hole in the fabric and count how many threads there are between this inch marker and the next inch marker. For example, if there are 18 threads in the counted area, then the fabric has 18 threads to the inch and is 18-count.

Canvas is an evenly woven, starched, cotton ground fabric; the holes between the threads are larger than the threads. Canvas is purchased by the count. Canvas is made up of multiple threads known as denier. The more denier per strands of canvas, the stronger the canvas; canvas with four or more denier is called deluxe canvas.

Mono Canvas is made of single, evenly woven vertical and horizontal threads that create uniform holes. Where the vertical and horizontal threads cross is an intersection. The intersections are free and can move with the stitching. The canvas can distort while being stitched but can be easily blocked back to shape (see page 104).

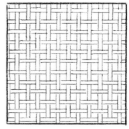

12-count mono canvas

Mono canvas comes in white, brown, and colors. When you're stitching on mono canvas, the *selvedge edges* should always be on the sides of the piece. This orientation makes the warps of the canvas run north and south and the weft threads of the canvas run east and west. Mono canvas counts range from 10 to 18.

Hint: Use brown mono canvas for projects with dark colors because it is difficult to cover white canvas fully with dark thread. Use colored mono canvas for designs that leave the ground fabric exposed to serve as an integral part of the pattern.

Hint: The "give" in mono canvas makes it a great choice for chair seats—the canvas moves with the body. Canvas types with locked intersections are more likely to give way and not withstand the wear as chair coverings.

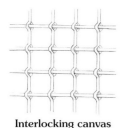

Interlocking canvas

Interlocking Canvas has single threads both vertically and horizontally, the same as mono canvas, but each intersection is locked—the warp threads are twisted around the weft threads so they cannot shift. Interlocking canvas is available in counts ranging from 5 to 18.

> **Hint:** Interlocking canvas is ideal for small projects such as ornaments because the canvas edges can be cut and will not ravel like mono canvas, making finishing easier.

Duo or Double Mesh Canvas has dual threads woven vertically and horizontally. The dual threads are counted both singly and doubly (6.5/13) for the canvas count. The dual warp threads (the ones running parallel to the selvedge) are woven closer together than the dual weft threads, which are woven a little further apart with a small opening present. Because of this unique weave, duo canvas is not a true evenweave canvas. The uneven weave makes it difficult to stitch diagonal stitches, but the dual threads give the stitcher the option of working over both threads for a large gauge or splitting the threads for a fine gauge. Duo canvas, also called Penelope canvas, is available in counts ranging from 6.5/13 to 14/28.

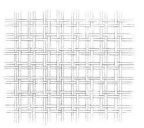

Duo canvas

Waste Canvas is a dual-weave canvas available with every tenth line a blue thread (called Blue Line) that facilitates counting or in solid white. Waste canvas is used to transfer a counted design onto an uncounted ground fabric. It is not for everyday canvas work—a little moisture will cause the canvas to come apart. Counts range from 6.5 to 16.

How Waste Canvas Works

To stitch a design from a counted cross-stitch chart on the front of a sweatshirt, cut a piece of waste canvas, baste it on the sweatshirt, stitch the counted pattern using the grid of the waste canvas. When all is stitched, dampen the waste canvas and pull out its threads, one by one, with tweezers. The result is a counted cross-stitch design on a fabric not intended for cross-stitch.

Plastic Canvas is a stable mesh made of plastic. It may be easily cut into shapes and washed and is ideal for children because of its stability. It's available in 10- or 14-count.

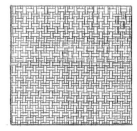

24-count Congress cloth

Congress Cloth is an evenweave fabric that is available highly starched for canvas work or with less starch for cross-stitch. It is 100% cotton and comes in white, light caramel, ivory, rose, pale blue, gray, and black. Congress cloth is available as 23- or 24-count.

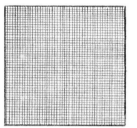

40-count silk gauze

Silk Gauze is a thin fabric for very fine silk, cotton, or other threads. Silk gauze has spaces between warp threads that allow the fabric to be counted, although it is not an evenweave fabric; the recommended stitch is continental. Always work silk gauze in a frame, never just in the hand. Counts available are 18, 32, and 40.

Aida Fabric is an evenweave fabric, ideal for counted cross-stitch. It's available in a wide variety of colors; 100% cotton, 100% wool, or a blend; in counts ranging from 6 to 22.

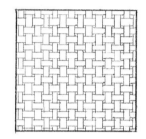

14-count Aida

PREPARING THE FABRIC

Prior to stitching, cover the raw edges of your ground fabric to keep them from raveling and getting caught in the stitching. For canvas, tape the edges or sew on bias binding; for other fabrics, zigzag or whip stitch the raw edges.

32-count linen

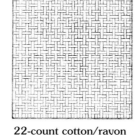

22-count cotton/rayon

Evenweave Linen Fabrics are available as 100% linen and a variety of blends in a wide spectrum of colors. Counts range from 14 to 45. Nonevenweave linens also come in a variety of colors and are ideal for surface embroidery and crewelwork.

DIRECTION OF STITCHING ON CANVAS

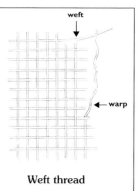

Projects will be more successful if you follow the direction or grain of the canvas. To stitch with the grain of the canvas, keep the selvedge edge on the east or west side of the stitching. The warp threads run north and south and the weft threads run east and west. When stitching in this manner, each stitch will lie flat and smooth with wide coverage. This is easy to do when the selvedges are visible, but if not, find the grain of the canvas by pulling one vertical and one horizontal thread completely out of the canvas. One will be more crinkled than the other—the warp thread. Turn the canvas so the crinkled threads are vertical (warp) and the smooth threads are horizontal (weft).

Weft thread

Care and Storage of Unstitched Fabrics

Most unstitched fabrics *should not be washed*; washing will remove the starch and make the fabric too limp. To store your unstitched fabrics, carefully roll up the fabric so the area to be stitched is on the inside. Roll acid-free tissue paper around the outside of the fabric and tie with a piece of soft yarn. **Do not store unstitched fabric in a tightly sealed plastic bag**; the fabric needs to breathe. Do store it in a closed, well-ventilated, dry area to keep dust away.

THREADS

Threads come in many sizes, colors, textures, and types; each has its function and adds to the enrichment of stitching. There are two basic categories of threads: stitchable and nonstitchable. A stitchable thread can be moved in and out of the ground fabric with ease and without damage to either. A nonstitchable thread cannot travel through the ground fabric and must be attached to the ground fabric with a second thread.

Definitions: **Ply** is a single length of wool, cotton, silk, or synthetic thread. **Strand** is two or more plies twisted together for strength. **Thread** is one or more strands of wool, cotton, silk, or synthetic. *Examples*: Cotton floss is six-stranded cotton made up of six strands, and each strand is made up of two plies. Persian yarn is three-stranded wool, and each strand is made up of two plies.

Stitchable Threads

WOOL THREADS

Persian yarn
3 strands, 2 plies each

Persian Yarn is a three-stranded, 100% wool thread that may be divided and worked in single or multiple strands. It comes in a great range of colors and families of color and can be purchased from some independent retailers by the individual strand—a great advantage when you have a project with 30 different colors and you need only a few strands of each color.

STRIPPING STRANDED THREADS

All stranded threads lie better if the strands are separated individually and then put back together for stitching. This action is called stripping the threads. Stripping the threads adds air between each strand and provides fuller coverage and smoother and more even stitches. As you make stitches, be sure that each strand is lying side by side on the fabric; avoid having one strand lying higher or twisting with another.

1. Take a single thread and hold it with your left fingers; let the thread hang down in a north-south direction.

2. With the fingers of your right hand, take 1 of the strands and pull it straight up and completely free from the remaining strands.

3. Lay this strand separately on a surface lying north to south.

4. Pull the next strand out and lay it next to the first strand and in the same direction.

5. Continue to pull each strand and add to the previous ones, always placing them in the same direction.

6. Combine the strands.

Hint: You may need less than all strands, so strip only the amount needed. Note for cotton thread: The strands may become knotted from the extraction of the first strand. If you do not straighten the strands before pulling the second strand, the thread becomes a tangled mess. Thread the north end in the needle and place a knot in the south end.

BUYING IN DYE LOTS

When doing a large background, be sure to purchase enough thread in the same dye lot—dye lots vary in color. This usually is not a problem when you're stitching a design area, but it is a problem when you're doing a solid background. The dye lot is usually printed on the thread label. Here are two tricks to use if you run out of thread with the same dye lot.

• Put the different dye lots in separate areas.

• If you don't have enough of one dye lot to complete a background, save the last few threads from the original dye lot and then mix strands of the original with strands of the new dye lot. This passage will form a stitched bridge between the two dye lots. When you have stitched the area with the mixed dye lot, continue stitching with the new dye lot; the change in lots will be almost undetectable.

**Tapestry yarn
single strand, 4 ply**

Tapestry Yarn is made of wool or a silk and wool combination. Tapestry yarn is a single twisted thread that is not separated. Wool tapestry thread is used primarily with 10-count canvas. Silk and wool tapestry thread fits comfortably in the holes of 14-count canvas.

Crewel Wool is a two-ply nonstrandable worsted soft wool used primarily for crewelwork on linen twill fabric. It also fits nicely on smaller size canvases and may be used as single or multiple threads. One strand of crewel wool is usually thinner than one strand of Persian wool.

TECHNIQUES FOR STITCHING WITH WOOL THREADS

- Always pull wool thread to the top of the work in one complete pull. Pulling with a jerky motion causes the wool to fuzz and pill and wears the thread.

- Use a large enough needle so the wool comes through the fabric cleanly. If the needle is too small, the wool will be roughed up by the fabric hole and will fuzz and pill.

- Whenever possible for needlepoint, come to the surface in empty holes and go down in filled holes to take the fuzz of the wool to the back of the work and keep the front surface smooth.

- Stitch each stitch with an even tension, the same small size, and in the same direction. No stitch should lie higher than another.

Floss
6 strands, 2 plies each

COTTON THREADS

Six-stranded cotton or floss is the most common 100% cotton thread and is available in a great range of colors.

Perle or Pearl Cotton is a softly twisted 100% cotton that comes in different sizes—12 is the smallest in diameter, 3 is the largest. Each skein or ball is identified with a size and number (the numbers correspond to the color numbers of six-strand cotton floss; this is helpful if you want a change of textures but desire the same color). Note: Not all colors of six-strand cotton floss are available in Perle Cotton.

Perle Cotton
Size 8

Stitching with Perle Cotton

Different sizes of Perle Cotton fit nicely into different sizes of needlepoint canvas.

Size	Stitch	Count/Fabric
5	diagonal	18/canvas
5 plus 1 or 2 strands of floss	upright	18/canvas
3	diagonal	14/canvas
3 plus 1 to 3 strands of floss	upright	14/canvas
8	diagonal	24/congress
12 cut in numerous lengths		any canvas

Hint: When combining Perle Cotton and floss, try using a different color of floss to produce special effects.

Overdyed Perle Cotton comes in size 5 and size 8. Some overdyed cottons (see page 32), single- and three-strand, come on cards accompanied by directions that explain what size to use on various ground fabrics.

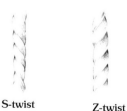

S-twist　　**Z-twist**

Perle Cottons are twisted threads. Twisted threads have either an *s*-twist or a *z*-twist. This is known as the *over-twist* of the thread. When you're stitching with a twisted thread, it is important to maintain the over-twist. Perle Cotton is an *s*-twisted thread.

DETERMINING AND MAINTAINING TWIST

Hold a strand of Perle Cotton. Spin the thread clockwise and see how the twist tightens. Spin the thread counterclockwise; the twist starts to open up and eventually comes untwisted. Return the thread to its original position and examine the twists; note approximately how many twists there are in 1 inch of thread. Don't go so far as to measure; you just want to become familiar with the twist. The normal action of stitching reduces the twists per inch. This twist reduction softens the thread and makes it fluffier and not as shiny; stitches become less crisp.

Here's how to halt this action: When you bring the needle to the surface of the ground fabric, spin the needle clockwise (for an s-twisted thread) to add back the over-twist that your stitching has eliminated. When you're just starting the thread and it's at its longest length, spin the thread every stitch. As the thread shortens, spin less and less.

If the thread starts to kink, you have too much over-twist on the thread. To relieve the kinking, take the needle to the back of the fabric and drop the needle; the over-twist will spin out. Maintaining a consistent over-twist makes stitches lie evenly and flat, and exhibit equal shine and tension.

Silk Threads

Silk has a natural beauty and can be dyed to achieve extraordinary color. Its natural luster is part of its makeup. Silk has a very smooth surface, which reflects light, and its somewhat translucent texture enhances the reflective powers. Silk is one of the strongest threads for stitching but it can wear by abrasion.

Stitching with Silk

To cut down on some of the abrasion, use a needle larger than necessary so the silk can slide through the hole cleanly. Never lay the silk on canvas to stroke with a laying tool (see page 40); doing so definitely will cause abrasions. Rough hands can form abrasions on the silk, so touch it as little as possible.

1. Always separate strands before stitching.

2. Always use a laying tool (see page 40) to make sure all the strands lie side by side.

3. Keep the silk up off the canvas when stitching.

4. Select stitches that show off the shine of the thread, stitches that turn different directions or have long-and-short combinations.

Silk thread comes from the cocoon of the silkworm. Two types of silk are used for needlework: reeled or flat silk and spun silk.

Reeled silk comes directly from the cocoon and is not spun; it is a continuous filament. Reeled silk is the most ambitious of silks to work with but it is wonderful to use on a silk ground fabric. Reeled silk threads predominate in Chinese and Japanese embroidery. Reeled silk will wear on canvas by abrasion and lose its luster, pill, and not lie smooth.

Spun silk is not a continuous filament. Lengths of silk are spun into strandable threads. Spun silk is much easier to stitch with than reeled silk. Silks can be tightly spun for a matted look or loosely spun for a shiny look. Tightly spun silk is the easiest to stitch with on canvas.

Floss Silks are 100% strandable silk, spun and softly twisted. Floss silk is not easy to work with on canvas (it tends to snag on the canvas), but it is worth it for the shine of the stitches. Floss silks make wonderful surface embroidery stitches on linen, silk, and cotton grounds.

Canvaswork Silks are more tightly spun and some are strandable (six-, seven-, eight-, or twelve-strand) and suitable for needlepoint. They are very easy to use and provide a play of light.

Linen Threads

Linen threads are suitable for both needlepoint, surface embroidery, and cross-stitch. They are nonstrandable.

Novelty Threads

Novelty threads are suitable for creating textures and special effects. There are fuzzy wool threads such as angora and alpaca, and soft wool such as Broider Wul often used for restoration work. Many of these novelty wools may be brushed for a true fur look. They work best in small decorative areas.

> **Hint:** Purchase several novelty threads. Using a blank piece of ground fabric, stitch an area with each thread. This fabric becomes a little notebook of stitches that shows how each novelty thread works.

Metallic Threads

Medium braid

Metallic threads are stitchable threads. The word *metallic* indicates that the content of the thread is not a real metal but a synthetic. (In contrast, metal threads are real gold or silver or a mixture of metals. Some are constructed with a silk or nylon core thread around which the metal is wrapped. Metal threads almost always are nonstitchable threads.)

Metallic threads add zip to needlework, such as a ribbon on a package, a border, stars in a dark night, crowns of gold, and so on. Metallic braids are very easy to stitch with and come in various diameters. Metallics also come as ribbons in several widths.

STITCHING WITH METALLIC THREADS

Some metallic threads have a tendency to ravel easily. To prevent the raveling, start with a shorter thread length (about 16 inches) and a needle 1 size larger than you would normally stitch with. The larger needle opens the fabric so the threads come through with minimal friction and rubbing and less tendency to ravel. Clip the end the minute it starts to ravel.

RAYONS

Rayons are available in skeins or on cards as stranded rayons, which need to be stripped before stitching. Nonstrandable rayon threads, which are twisted, are available as well.

Rayon threads provide a play of light and are festive enhancements. Rayon ribbons, which seem to widen on big canvases and compress on small canvases, are available as well. A laying tool is critical when you're working with rayon ribbon.

Hint: Run a damp cloth or new make-up sponge along rayon thread prior to stitching to make stitching easier.

Nonstitchable Threads

A nonstitchable thread is one that does not stand up to the wear and tear of coming up and down through the fabric ground. An example is Japanese Gold or Silver. Nonstitchable threads are also termed **couchable** threads. Couching is the manner in which a thread of any thickness is attached to the ground fabric with another different and usually finer thread. The fine thread can form a decorative pattern while holding the thick thread to the ground fabric or it can be stitched at repeat intervals. You can obtain beautiful curves and straight lines by couching (see page 76). When you're couching on canvas, the couching stitches do not adhere to the grid of the canvas.

THREAD COVERAGE

On canvas, an upright stitch takes one strand more for coverage than a stitch that covers an intersection.

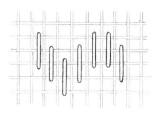

Upright stitch

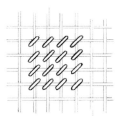

Diagonal stitch

PERSIAN WOOL COVERAGE

COUNT/FABRIC	# OF STRANDS/STITCH
18/canvas	1/diagonal 2/upright
14 or 12/canvas	2/diagonal 3/upright
10/canvas	3/diagonal 4 or 5/upright

Note: Dark colors of wool are usually thinner (due to the dyeing process) than light colors. For full coverage, you may have to use additional strands of dark colors.

Hint: In needlepoint, black or darker colors of wool may not cover a white canvas fully even if you add an additional strand, and adding that strand may make the stitching too thick. Here are two tips: Add a single strand of floss the exact color of the Persian wool or paint the canvas with acrylic paint (allow to dry completely before stitching).

CREWEL WOOL COVERAGE

COUNT/FABRIC	# OF STRANDS/STITCH
18/canvas or linen	1/diagonal 2/upright
14/canvas or linen	2/diagonal 3/upright
12/canvas or linen	3/diagonal 4/upright
10/canvas or linen	4 or 5/diagonal 5 or 6/upright

Six-stranded Cotton (Floss) Coverage

Count/Fabric	# of Strands/Stitch
36 or 32/linen	1
28/linen	1 or 2
25 or 24/evenweave	2
24/Congress cloth	2 or 3/diagonal 3 or 4/upright
22/Hardanger	2
18/canvas	3 or 4/diagonal 5 or 6/upright
18/Aida	2
18/linen	2 or 3
14/canvas	5 or 6/diagonal 6 or 7/upright
14/Aida	3
12/canvas	6 or 7/diagonal 7 or 8/upright

SILK THREAD COVERAGE

COUNT/FABRIC	# OF STRANDS/STITCH
40/silk	1/diagaonal
18/canvas	3 or 4/diagonal 4 or 5/upright
14/canvas	4 or 5/diagonal 6 or 7/upright
12/canvas	7 or 8/diagonal 8 or 9/upright
10/canvas	8 or 9/diagonal 9 or 10/upright

Note: The above amounts are only suggestions. The diameter of the threads in the ground fabric may vary and may require a different number of strands. Amounts for blank canvases differ from the amounts required for handpainted canvases (the paint adds thickness to the canvas threads, making the holes slightly smaller). Experiment with the number of strands on your chosen ground fabric before you begin your project.

Color

Most threads come in families of color that run from a very dark value of the hue to a very light value. **Hue** is the name of the color—red, green, etc.—in its purest form. For example, the hue of red goes from a deep reddish black to the palest pink. **Value** is the change from lightness to darkness of the hue. It is this light-dark contrast that makes the shading of the petals of a flower so successful.

Hint: A design will appear very unbalanced if it employs all deep values or all light values. Make sure you have a variety of lightness and darkness.

CHANGING COLORS

It's easy to change colors in designs by using the value scale. On a value scale, the lightest value is numbered 1 (in the case of red, palest pink). The darkest value is numbered 9 (reddish black). All numbers between 1 and 9 mirror the steps that occur when different amounts of black and white are mixed.

Find the colors that the design calls for (it is helpful to have the skeins in hand of the actual colors). For example, the design has a rose in four values—a light, medium, medium dark, and dark—of yellow, and you prefer pink. Choose four pinks whose values match those of the yellow. You can substitute any color for another and have it work in the design if you swap value for value.

Some threads are ***variegated***. The hue of the thread ranges from a light value to a dark value in a repeated sequence. Variegated threads work especially well in darning patterns for creating the effect of grass or sky.

Some threads are ***overdyed*** or redyed with darker or lighter values of the original color or with a different color—primarily silk, cotton, and wool. Overdyed threads work well for skies, grasses, leaves, and creative effects. Dye lots vary greatly in overdyes, so be sure to purchase enough thread to finish the project.

NEEDLES

There are many kinds of needles: tapestry for wool or stranded threads on canvas, chenille with a sharp point for ease in getting through fabrics or couching, embroidery or crewel with an elongated eye for threading stranded threads, darners for mending, milliners with a longer length than a general sewing needle, quilting with a shortened length, and sharps for general sewing. Each is available in a variety of sizes.

Tapestry Needles are used for most needlepoint and counted cross-stitch. The large eye accommodates wool or stranded threads and the blunt end allows the needle to go through the ground fabric smoothly. The higher the number the smaller the needle, and sizes range from 28 (smallest) to 13 (largest).

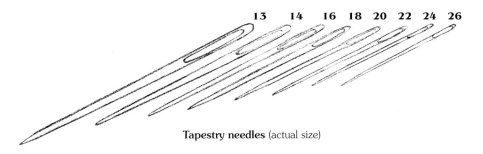

Tapestry needles (actual size)

APPROPRIATE TAPESTRY NEEDLE SIZES

NEEDLE SIZE	CANVAS COUNT	COUNTED CROSS-STITCH FABRIC
18	10	7 or 8 threads to the inch
20	12	10 threads to the inch
22	14	11-count Aida
22	16	14-count Aida
22	18	16-count Aida
24	22	
24	24 Congress	18–25 threads to the inch
26		25–32 threads per inch
28		36–40 threads per inch

How to Determine if the Needle is the Right Size

You can tell if your needle is too large for the ground fabric by moving the threaded needle up through an unstitched hole. If the threaded needle enlarges the hole, it is too large. It should come through the hole cleanly without making the size of the hole bigger. But there are times when you must break this rule: If you're stitching with a delicate thread such as angora, which tends to wear with repeated stitching, use a large needle to open up the hole so the soft threads flow along without damage.

Using a needle that is too small will pinch the thread and make it "skinny." In the case of stranded threads, a needle that is too small will prevent loft and the threads will lie too close together. When in doubt, err on the large side.

Chenille Needles are suitable for most surface and ribbon embroidery and follow the same numbering and size as the tapestry needle but have a sharp point. Chenille needles come in handy for stitching with a thread, stranded rayon for example, that is disturbed by going into or coming up in a shared hole in canvas. The needle cuts through the thread in the hole rather than moving it aside and disturbing the stitch.

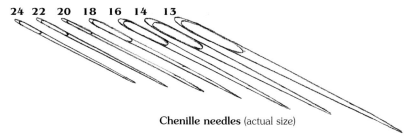

Chenille needles (actual size)

Couching Needles are small and sharp needles used for couching down a thread; the needle should be able to pierce the stitching. A size 9 or 10 crewel needle is a good choice.

Holding the Needle

When you're stitching with any needle, carefully feel the needle on the underside of the work. *Hold the eye of the needle between your thumb and forefinger* and bring the needle to the top of your work so you can *see through the eye of the needle*. Following this procedure brings the thread up in the proper direction to make a stitch.

Once the needle clears the fabric, take it *straight up* for the full length of the thread. While the thread is extended to its full length, take a small pull on the thread. This will ensure the thread is *set* (or tight) on the back of the work.

Hint: Keep needles in a container. A magnetic box with the needles sorted by sizes and types works well.

Flip the needle over in your fingers in preparation to taking it back down through the fabric. *It should go down through the fabric in the*

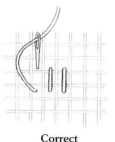

Correct

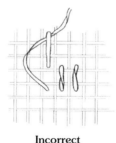

Incorrect

Hint: Needles are not marked, so it can be hard to determine size. To help, place one of every size on a small piece of felt so when in doubt you can compare.

same position that it came up. This technique helps to prevent the threads from twisting so they will lie exactly where you want them. It also provides an even tension for your stitches.

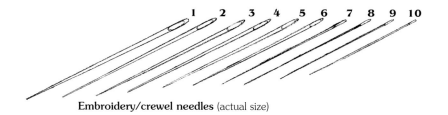

Embroidery/crewel needles (actual size)

CARING FOR NEEDLES

- The acid in skin can cause needles to turn black; if this happens, dust your hands with pure talc before stitching to absorb the acid.

- Any rust on needles will come off on your work. Discard rusted needles.

- Avoid using a sterling silver needle or thimble; the patina will rub off on your work.

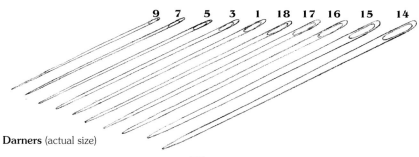

Darners (actual size)

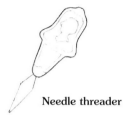

Needle threader

Needle Threader

A needle threader can come in handy.
Keep a couple with your needles or make
one with a piece of paper.

MAKE A NEEDLE THREADER

Cut a small piece of paper ½ inch wide by 1 inch
long. Fold the paper in half and insert the thread
end(s) into the fold of the paper. Thread the
paper through the needle's eye; pull the paper all
the way through the eye. Your thread comes
through the eye with the paper.

Making a needle threader

*Illustrations of actual-size needles based
on needles courtesy of the Colonial Needle Company.*

TOOLS

Scissors

Proper scissors are very important. **Embroidery** scissors about 4 inches long with a very sharp point and sharp blades are best. The sharp point is necessary for cutting out unwanted stitches and cutting off thread ends. The 4-inch length is a comfortable fit for most hands; larger scissors are awkward to handle and will not get in close enough to the fabric to snip off loose ends.

Embroidery scissors

Do not use your scissors for any purpose other than cutting nonmetallic threads. Using them to cut metallic threads or paper will dull them. Keep a separate pair of scissors on hand just for metallic threads.

Do not put a thread or ribbon on your embroidery scissors and hang them around your neck. You can jab yourself seriously when the scissors are in this position.

Also very handy are **clipper** scissors for hard-to-reach small threads and knots. A pinching motion cuts the threads. These scissors come with a cap that slips over the blades.

Clipper scissors

Lights and Lamps

A good cool **white light** makes all work clear. **Magnifying lamps** are very helpful when you're working with fine fabrics.

Laying Tools

A laying tool, used to lay threads flat and straight, is an essential aid. Controlling the thread completely on the front of the work as well as on the back is the only way to lay stitches correctly. The thread should lie flat, and all strands should be even, side by side, and resemble a ribbon. There should be no open space from one stitch to another. The laying tool has a sharp point for laying the threads across, with the other end squared so it does not roll off the work.

Laying tool

Hint: A laying tool is perfect for "reverse" stitching; the sharp point makes it easy to pick out errant stitches.

Using a Laying Tool

1. Bring the threaded needle straight up to the front of the ground fabric until the thread is taut, making sure of the position of the needle's eye (see page 35.) If the thread is twisted, spin the needle between the thumb and forefinger to eliminate the extra twist. Tug the thread sharply to tighten (set) the stitch on the back of your work.

2. Take the needle down through the fabric while gently holding the threads off the ground fabric with your other hand. When there is approximately 2 inches of thread on the surface of the canvas, insert the laying tool into the loop and gently stroke the thread in the direction of the stitch only. The thread should need only two or three strokes to straighten the strands so they enter the fabric side by side and with equal tension.

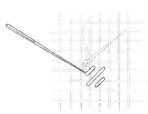

Stroking the thread with the laying tool

3. Complete the stitch, holding the needle tight on the underside of the fabric to maintain tension. Place the laying tool on the base of the stitch to hold the stitch in place.

4. While you're holding the stitch in place with the laying tool, poke the needle up through the fabric for the next stitch. Leaving the needle suspended, put the laying tool down and stop the action. With the other hand on the back, take hold of the thread on the back and pull gently to keep the tension on the existing stitch. With the hand on top, pick up the needle and pull the thread up. Maintain the tension on the thread on the back with the other hand during this upward motion. When the thread is completely at the top, run your fingers along the underside of the work to make sure it is flat and unknotted, and then take an extra tug on the thread to set the stitch.

Holding the stitch with the laying tool

LAYING TOOL HINTS

• It is just as important to lay and tighten the thread on the back of the work as on the front.

• Stroking back and forth will cause the thread to fuzz. Stroke only in the direction of the stitch.

• If the strands are not straightened in 2 or 3 strokes, check to make sure the thread was not brought up twisted or twisted when going down to the back of the fabric.

LAYING TOOLS—WHAT COULD BE WRONG?

If one strand rolls on the top of another in your stitch, take the stitch out and re-lay it. Here are some reasons why this might happen (and it will when you are first learning):

1. The thread was not straightened enough. *Solution*: Make sure the thread is not twisted when you bring it to the front of the fabric.

2. The laying tool isn't exerting even tension. *Solution*: Make sure all strands are evenly placed on the tool.

3. One strand has less tension than the others in the stitch. *Solution*: Make sure each strand is not twisted.

4. There are too many strands in your needle. *Solution*: Eliminate a strand.

TRANSFERRING A DESIGN

It is very important to use a **permanent pen** any time you mark on canvas or fabric. Do not trust the pen even if it is advertised indelible or permanent. Test it. First darken in a half-inch area of the ground fabric. Stitch over the darkened area with white thread. Submerge the stitched area in water. Do not use the pen if the ink comes off on the white thread or if the ink wicks out into adjacent areas of the ground fabric. If you choose to mark in color, test each color.

Soft pencils, #2, leave a residue on the fabric that comes off on the threads. For short lines or to mark a center that you do not want too dark, mark with a #4 hard pencil; it will not soil thread.

TRANSFERRING TO CANVAS

Tape the design to be transferred to a sunny window. Tape the blank canvas on top of the design. Trace over the design lines onto the canvas. A light table will work even better.

> **Hint:** Micron Pigma Pens, available at office supply stores or art stores, work well. They come in black and colors and in different sizes. Try a size 08 to mark on canvas and size 005 for fabric.

> **Hint:** When you're marking lines on canvas, make the narrowest line possible. The line will need to be covered fully with thread, and a narrow line is easier to cover. Heavy dark lines can shadow through a work, especially when you're using light-colored thread.

If desired, areas may be colored in with colored pens or acrylic paints. If you're using acrylics, do not fill the holes with paint (if necessary, thin the paint with water). Clogged holes will wear the thread.

TRANSFERRING TO FABRIC

Transfer paper: Place the transfer paper on the ground fabric. Place the design on top of the transfer paper. Using a narrow-point awl or stylist, trace the design lines onto the ground fabric.

Tissue paper: Copy the design onto tissue paper. Place the tissue paper on the right side of the fabric. Hold the tissue paper in place with pins, basting stitches, or pairs of magnets. With one strand of couching-weight thread, stitch each line of the design with a running stitch. Keep the stitches very close together, with very little of the stitches on the back of the work. Once all the lines of the design have been stitched, very carefully tear the paper away.

Hint: The advantage to the tissue-paper method is that there are no marks on the ground fabric, and if a line needs to be moved, the stitching can be picked out and a new line stitched without leaving a residual mark.

MOUNTING FABRIC

Most fabrics should be mounted on a roller frame, stretcher bars, or in an embroidery hoop prior to stitching. The *mounting helps maintain an even tension* on the fabric and stitches.

   Cross-stitch fabric may be placed in a hoop, sewn on to a roller frame, or *stitched in your hand*. To stitch in your hand, place your left hand under the ground fabric with your forefinger and middle finger under the area that you are stitching to support the fabric as you stitch. With the right hand, make your stitches with a sewing motion, going in and out of the ground fabric in an even and fluid motion. The left two fingers always remain under the stitching to support the fabric; use the left thumb to smooth the stitches or hold the thread. This also works well for pieces that are too large for a roller frame or ones you do not want multiply hoop marks on the fabric.

Mounting on a Roller Frame

1. Determine the size of the design—called the design size.

2. Cut the fabric 3 inches larger on all 4 sides—called the fabric size. This is a very important distinction. The extra fabric around the design size is used for making a pillow, framing the piece, or blocking the piece back in shape.

3. With a permanent marker (see page 43), mark the selvedge sides east and west. Mark the two remaining sides, one

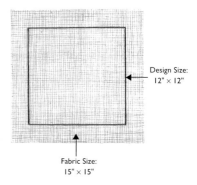

Design Size:
12" × 12"

Fabric Size:
15" × 15"

north/top and one south/bottom. By marking the fabric in this manner you will be stitching with the grain of the fabric, i.e., the warp threads are vertical and the weft threads are horizontal (see page 15).

4. If you're using canvas, tape the east and west edges of the canvas; if you're using fabric, tape or zigzag the edges. (If one of these two sides has a selvedge, it is not necessary to tape that side.) Place half the tape along the front edge of the fabric. Cut the tape to fit and finger press in place. Turn the fabric over and fold the other half of the tape to the backside. Press with firm pressure to ensure that the tape adheres to the fabric. Do not tape the north or the south edges.

> **Hint:** For taping canvas, 2-inch-wide white artist tape or strapping tape works well; masking tape does not stick as well.

5. Measure the north and south edges and mark the center on both edges with a pencil.

6. Find and mark the center of the twill tape on both twill-taped bars that are supplied with the roller frame.

7. Line up the center of the twill-taped bar with the center north raw edge of the fabric. Place the fabric under the twill tape (the fabric will be between the tape and the wooden rod). *Note: Do not put the fabric on top of the twill tape. Putting it on top will not create the proper tension on the fabric, and threads will constantly snag on the raw edge of the fabric.*

8. Turn the fabric over so the wrong side is up (the fabric will be visible on the tape).

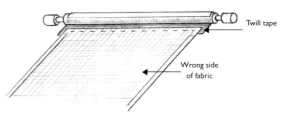

Fabric on a roller frame

9. Pin the fabric in place with a few straight pins, and then sew, by hand or machine, all the way across. If fabric, sew straight across the same thread; if canvas, sew along the same row of canvas holes (this ensures even tension on the fabric when it is stretched tight on the frame). Back stitch both ends to lock the stitches. If you're sewing by hand, use a double strand of ordinary sewing thread or a single strand of carpet or buttonhole thread using a back stitch to secure in place.

10. Attach the south side of the fabric to the twill tape in the same manner.

11. Insert the tape-rods into the end bars.

12. Turn the north bar until the fabric is in a position to start stitching; firmly tighten the two top bolts.

13. Turn the south bar until all the slack is out of the fabric, and then give it an extra turn so that the fabric is drum-tight; firmly tighten the bolts.

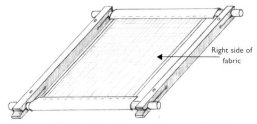

Fabric placed correctly in a roller frame

Hint: It is perfectly all right to roll up the worked areas in the frame.

Hint: At any time, the bolts may be loosened to roll the fabric to a new position for stitching.

Hint: Each time you start to work, test the fabric; it should be drum-tight. If not, loosen either the top two bolts or bottom two bolts and take the excess slack out of the work by turning the dowel.

For a very large piece or a piece that needs to be extra tight, lace the edges of the fabric after the fabric has been placed on the frame. Carpet or buttonhole thread is strong enough to withstand the tension of the lacing.

To remove the piece from the roller frame, cut the stitches that secured the canvas to the twill tape. A seam ripper is very handy for this job. *Do not cut the twill tape*; it is reusable.

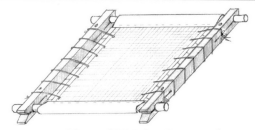

Mounted fabric laced

Stretcher Bars

Fabric may be stapled to artist stretcher bars, available at art supply stores, with a staple gun or attached with extra-long tacks (ordinary tacks are usually not deep enough). Stretcher bars are sold in pairs, so for an 18-inch-by-18-inch piece of fabric, purchase two 18-inch pairs.

1. Put the two pairs together to form a square.

2. Mark the center on all four sides of the stretcher bars.

3. Tape or whip stitch the four sides of the fabric.

4. Mark the center on all four sides of the fabric and line them up with the marks on the stretcher bars.

5. Place a tack or staple in the four center spots. Continue to place tacks or staples out from the center on one side until that side is completely attached. Move to an adjacent side and do the same thing, moving out from the center and pulling the fabric taut; repeat until all four sides of the fabric are tacked or stapled to the stretcher strips.

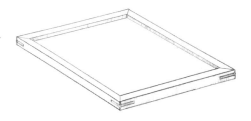

Stretcher bars

Hint: As stitching progresses, the fabric will become loose and spongy in the center. Pull out the staples or tacks and reattach so the fabric is drum-tight. Do not try to tighten just by adding more staples or tacks; all must be removed and redone. The work should be tight at all times.

Embroidery Hoops

Evenweave fabrics such as linen, Aida cloth, Hardanger, and nonevenweave fabrics such as silk, cotton, and blends may be mounted in an embroidery hoop. Hoops come in a variety of sizes ranging from 2- to 12-inches wide and are made of wood, plastic, or metal.

Embroidery hoop

MOUNTING IN A HOOP

1. Lay the hoop flat on a hard surface and loosen the screw enough so that the outer hoop comes off. Set the outer hoop aside.

The fabric over the inner hoop

Hint: For embroidery, a wooden or plastic hoop with a screw mechanism to tighten the hoop, which makes the fabric very tight, works well. The fingertips should be able to reach the center of the fabric in the hoop with ease. If you can't reach the center, it becomes harder to hold the hoop and perform the stitches. If you use a large hoop (over 8-inches wide), secure it to a table with a clamp or weight to free up your hands.

2. Lay the fabric over the inner hoop, positioning it where stitching will begin.

3. Place the outer hoop on top of the fabric. Push the outer hoop down until it completely fits around the inner hoop.

4. Tighten the screw a bit; stop; pull the fabric to take out any slack. Tighten the screw a bit more, and then pull the fabric again. Repeat until the hoop is tight and the fabric is stretched drum-tight.

The outer hoop on the fabric

> **Hint:** To prevent hoop marks on already stitched areas, place several layers of tissue paper over the fabric, and then push the outer hoop down on the paper, fabric, and inner hoop. When tight, tear the paper away from the stitching area.

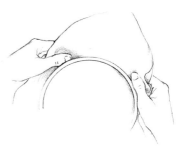

The fabric stretched in the hoop

> **Hint:** To prevent damage to delicate fabrics, wrap the two parts of the hoop in strips of cotton before securing the fabric.

The Stab Method

Never try to stitch with a sewing motion in a hoop. Always work with one hand on the bottom supporting the hoop, and the other hand on the top plying the needle. This technique is called the ***stab method***.

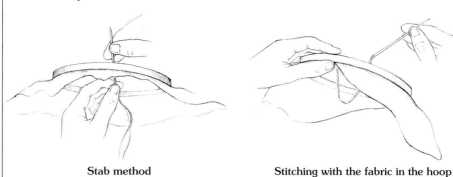

Stab method   Stitching with the fabric in the hoop

STARTING A THREAD

There are several ways to start a thread. All may be used on any type of ground fabric. Depending on the stitch, some work better than others.

Waste Knot

1. Thread the needle. Place a small knot in the end of the thread and cut off any extra thread hanging off the knot.

2. Place the knot on top of the fabric in the path that the stitching will travel, about 1 inch from the starting stitch.

3. Place a pinhead stitch (see next page) before making the first stitch.

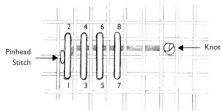

Placement of a waste knot

4. Take the first stitch approximately 1 inch from the knot. Stitch toward the knot, covering the thread running from the knot to the first stitch on the back and the pinhead stitch.

5. When your stitching reaches the knot, snip the knot off. ***When you're snipping the knot off, turn the tip of the scissors away from the stitching.*** Nothing is worse than cutting the knot and the stitching at the same time. The tail of the thread will have been covered on the back by the stitching.

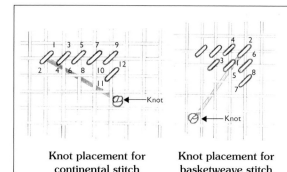

Knot placement for continental stitch

Knot placement for basketweave stitch

Hint: The waste knot is the conventional method of starting when you're using any of the tent stitch variations on canvas. Place the knot at an angle to the row of stitching if you're stitching across in straight rows of continental stitch; covering the tail of the thread in just one row might raise that row slightly and make a ridge on the front of the work. Place the knot straight across from the first stitch if you're stitching diagonal rows in the diagonal tent (basketweave) stitch.

Pinhead Stitch

A pinhead stitch puts the proper tension on the starting thread. Bring the needle to the front of the work. Bring the needle up and then down in a hole next door, either vertically or horizontally, but not over an intersection. This movement makes a small stitch that will cover one thread of the fabric and disappear into the fabric. It will be stitched over when you stitch this area.

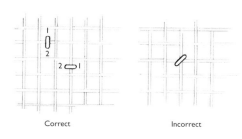

Correct   Incorrect

Pinhead stitch placement

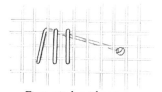

First stitch without a pinhead

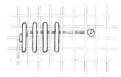

First stitch with a pinhead

Hint: *When you're stitching any* upright stitch (for example, Gobelin or satin stitch), after placing the knot on the right side of the work, make a pinhead stitch under the first intended stitch before you start that stitch. The pinhead stitch ensures that the first stitch will be straight; *otherwise the first stitch will slant toward the knot.*

Away Waste Knot

1. Place a knot at the end of the thread and cut off any extra thread.

2. Place the knot on the top of the work, at least 6 or 7 inches away from the starting stitch. After you have done some stitching, clip off the top of the knot.

3. Turn the work over and thread the tail in the needle. Weave the tail in and out of the stitched area for a distance of at least 1 inch.

4. Clip off excess thread.

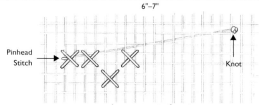

Away waste knot

Hint: The away waste knot is good for stitches that are very sparse or open and/or when you cannot guarantee that the distance from the thread to the knot will be covered completely. This knot works successfully for pulled thread, blackwork, whitework, and shadow work, because the thread can be woven along the path of stitching and miss the open areas.

"L" Stitch

1. Place a knot in the end of thread. Cut off excess thread.

2. Place the knot on the surface of the work 1 inch from the starting point.

3. Make an "L" stitch (actually two stitches: one is stitched over one thread horizontally and one is stitched over one thread vertically; both stitches will share the same hole).

4. Clip the waste knot from the surface. The "L" stitch is not removed; stitch right over it.

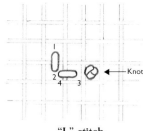

"L" stitch

> **Hint:** The "L" stitch starting method will work very well for decorative stitches and slippery threads, such as rayon. If you're using a textured or metallic thread, the "L" stitch may not work well under an area stitched in continental or basketweave.

½-Thread Method

This is appropriate for working with a very long thread such as in a blackwork pattern or whitework techniques where it is hard to start and finish off threads.

1. Thread one end of a long length of thread in the needle; do not knot the other end of the thread.

2. Take the needle down through the ground fabric in the center of where the stitching will begin.

3. Bring the needle up next door and pull the thread so half the thread is on one side of that stitch and half the thread is on the other side of that stitch.

4. Make a pinhead stitch to secure this first stitch.

5. Thread the left half of the thread into the needle and stitch leftward to the end. End the thread the same as an away waste knot.

6. Repeat for the right half.

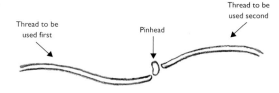

½-Thread method

Knot on the Back

It is the conventional wisdom that threads are never started by putting a knot on the back of the work (knots can leave a large lump on the back; during framing or finishing the lump will appear on the front side). The rule applies unless you're starting a *very thin thread* such as a couching thread or one strand of six-strand cotton. For most fabrics, a waste knot made with the very tiny thread will pull right through the fabric.

1. Place a single knot in the end of the thread; cut off excess thread.

2. Place the knot on the back of the work; bring the threaded needle to the front of the fabric; work a pinhead stitch; and progress.

Starting a Couching Thread

Couching threads are very fine and any knots tend to slip through the ground fabric. Here's how to avoid the problem.

1. Thread the needle.

2. Place a single knot in the end of the thread; cut off any extra thread.

3. Place the knot on the back of the ground fabric and come up. If you're working on canvas, Aida, or any counted ground fabric, pierce a thread on the upward motion and go back down through the nearest hole. If you're working on satin, linen, silk, or any uncounted ground fabric, make a pinhead stitch on the front of the fabric in an area to be covered with stitches. (See page 76 for more on couching.)

ENDING A THREAD

When you approach the end of the stitching thread, it needs to be affixed. There are several ways to end the thread; all are appropriate for all types of ground fabrics.

Weaving In

The conventional method is to turn the work over to the back and weave the thread into a stitched area. Weaving back through must be done with great care because it produces a thick, somewhat matted back. Here are some tips:

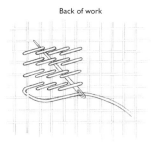

Back of work

Weaving in on diagonal rows

• Weave so as not to disturb the stitches on the front.

• If the stitches were *stitched in horizontal rows, weave the thread in the back on diagonal rows.* This assures that one row of holes on the back aren't lifted, which will result in tightening them on the front and causing a ridge in the finished area.

> **Hint:** Weaving the thread on diagonal rows works well for stitches such as mosaic, cashmere, upright Gobelin, brick, interlocking Gobelin, Hungarian, Parisian, alternating continental, and continental.

- If the stitches were stitched in diagonal rows, weave the thread back in straight rows, either vertical or horizontal.

Hint: Weaving the thread in straight rows works well for the diagonal tent stitch (basketweave).

Back of work vertically

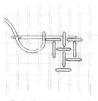

Back of work horizontally

Weaving in on straight rows

Waste Ending

1. Bring the thread to the surface of the fabric about 1 inch from the last stitch and in the path that the stitching will travel.

2. Thread a new needle and continue stitching.

3. Stitch toward the thread end and when close to the thread end, clip off. Thin, slippery threads should be knotted on the surface with a French knot to prevent them from slipping out.

← Thread end

← French knot

Waste ending

Pinhead Ending

1. Bring the needle up through the stitching to make a part or opening in the stitched area.

2. Take the needle back down in the same opening, making sure the stitch goes over one thread of the ground fabric.

3. Pull the thread tight on the back of the work; the part or opening will close and the pinhead stitch will become invisible.

4. Make a second pinhead stitch close to the first one.

5. Bring the thread to the front of the work close to the last pinhead stitch, and cut off the thread on top of the work.

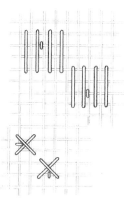

Pinhead stitches in worked areas

Hint: The pinhead method allows you to stop and start in an area, then go on to a new color without carrying the new color through the old color. It works very well for all stitches except the three tent-stitch variations or very heavy metallic threads such as a #16 braid. It's really helpful when you're stitching with 30 or 40 colors or need to change color often.

PINHEAD STITCHES

How can pinhead stitches hold the work successfully? Make two pinhead stitches and then try to pick them out!

"L" Stitch

1. Bring the needle to the top of the fabric into an area that will be stitched later.

2. Make an "L" stitch (see page 56).

3. Make a second "L" stitch near the first.

> **Hint:** The "L" stitch ending works well with rayon and rayon ribbons, i.e., threads that are slippery. If the thread is too slippery make a French knot in the tail and leave until the stitching reaches the knot, then clip the knot off.

4. Bring the end of the thread to the top of the fabric close to the second "L" stitch.

5. Leave the end on top of the fabric until stitching starts to cover the distance between stitching and the hanging thread; then cut off the end of the thread.

Whipping Down Threads

Use the whipping-down method for decorative threads such as ribbons or metal and metallic threads.

> **Hint:** It is very important to use a small needle (size 10 or 9 crewel) when whipping down threads, so that the stitching on the front of the fabric is not disturbed.

1. Thread a very small, sharp needle with 1 strand of cotton floss or couching thread.

2. Place a small single knot in the end of the floss or thread, cut off any excess thread; and weave the knot into the back of the work.

3. Carefully whip stitch, 3 or 4 times, the thread to the back of a stitched area.

4. Run the needle through a loop of the stitching thread to make a small knot and cut off.

SINKING NEEDLE

A sinking needle is used to **take a nonstitchable or stray thread to the back** of the work on any ground fabric. It also may be used as a starting or ending method for any thread.

1. Using a size 24 chenille needle, thread 24 inches of strong cotton such as buttonhole thread or size 8 or 12 Perle Cotton through the eye of the needle. Place the needle in the middle of the thread.

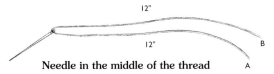

Needle in the middle of the thread

2. Securely anchor the needle and the thread-end marked A in the diagram by having someone hold both or placing the needle securely in the ground fabric and holding the thread-end marked A in your teeth.

3. Place thread-end marked B at the base of the palm of your right hand (the needle is still in the middle of the thread and securely held). Hold thread-end B in place with the fingertips of your left hand (Figure 1).

4. Roll your left fingertips up your right palm (Figures 2 and 3). Roll the length of your two hands. The thread will end in the palm of your left hand (Figure 4).

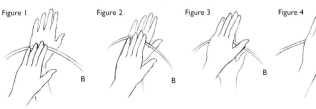

5. Repeat this process a second time on the same hand. This is under-twisting the thread.

6. Replace thread-end B with thread-end A while maintaining the twist on B and tension on both ends. Repeat the procedure using thread-end A.

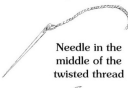

Needle in the middle of the twisted thread

7. Take both thread ends and place them together at the base of your left palm and with the fingertips of your right hand, roll up your left hand. Repeat. This is termed *over-twisting the thread*. The result is **a twisted thread with the needle caught in the middle** of the twisted thread.

Loop

8. Thread the twisted thread back through the needle's eye to form a loop. (The loop will take starting, ending, and stray threads to the back of the ground fabric.)

Needle through the fabric with the loop on top of the fabric

9. Insert the needle in the ground fabric at the precise point that you wish to take the thread to the back of the work, leaving the loop on top of the fabric.

Loop around the thread to be sunk

10. Place the loop around the thread to be sunk (thread should be no longer than ½ inch; sink threads 1 at a time).

First thread has been sunk

11. With a quick downward motion on the needle, pull the loop through to the back of the work. The *loop will automatically close like a noose* and "pop" the thread to the back neatly.

12. Once the threads have been sunk to the back, secure them to the back: Turn the work to the back, bend the threads over against the back of the ground fabric; with couching thread, whip the threads into the back of the work; run the needle through a loop of thread to make a small knot and cut off the end.

> **Hint:** Use a small size 9 or 10 crewel needle to secure the threads to the back of the work so that the stitching on the front is not disturbed.

STARTING TO STITCH

Thread Length

Thread length depends on personal preference and the type of thread used. Here are some general guidelines.

Thread	Length in Inches
Perle Cotton	18
Silk (tightly spun)	20
Cotton floss	18
Novelty threads	15–18
Metallics	16

Threading the Needle

Fold the thread over the needle to form a very tight crease. Pull the needle out, leaving the creased thread between your thumb and forefinger. You should barely see the thread between your fingers. If

Threading a needle

you see too much thread, then it is not taut enough. Slide the needle's eye over the creased thread. Move the needle back and forth a little to engage all the thread. Gently pull on the thread and bring it through the eye. If you have trouble, use a needle threader (see page 38).

Where to Start

• When stitching a piece with the design already in place, start with the foreground area first.

• In cross-stitch, start with a corner or the place where starting to count the design will be the easiest.

CHOOSING THE RIGHT STITCH

For small areas, choose a small stitch with an easy-to-repeat pattern, not one with a large repeat pattern. For areas that need to have a textured look—bushes, trees, Santa's coat, animals—try a simple stitch with a thread that is fuzzy or shiny. Most of the stitch diagrams featured in this book are grouped by areas appropriate for their use.

Different stitches add texture and interest, especially when you're stitching a painted canvas in needlepoint.

The best advice: Try a stitch and/or thread; if you don't like the effect, take it out. Keep a notebook with stitch diagrams and threads that work well for certain areas.

THE STITCHES

The conventional stitch for **needlepoint** (canvas work) is the **tent stitch.** The conventional stitch for **counted cross-stitch** is the **cross-stitch.** All tent stitches are one-half of a cross-stitch.

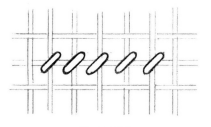

Tent stitch

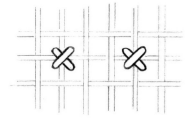

Cross-stitch

The *tent stitch is a family of three stitches*: Two are stitched in horizontal rows—the continental and the half-cross-stitch—and the third is stitched in diagonal rows—the diagonal tent or basketweave. The three stitches appear the same on the front of the work but there are distinct differences on the back.

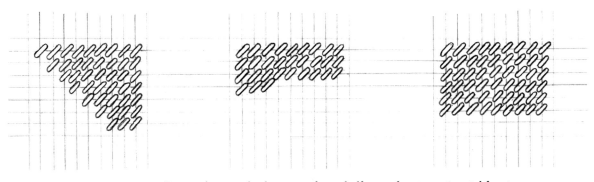

LEFT TO RIGHT: **Diagonal tent or basketweave front, half-cross front, continental front**

To tell the difference between the three stitches, turn the work over to the back.

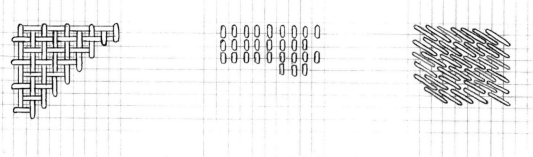

LEFT TO RIGHT: Diagonal tent or basketweave back, half-cross back, continental back

Hint: Any stitch worked on canvas must go under two canvas threads on the back of the canvas to lock the stitch in place. The half-cross stitch does not go under two canvas threads on mono canvas. Therefore, use the half-cross stitch on dual canvas. Use the continental or basketweave stitch on mono canvas.

Hint: Needlepoint wears from the back of the work long before it wears from the front of the work. The fuller back on the continental or basketweave provides for a longer life for the needlepoint.

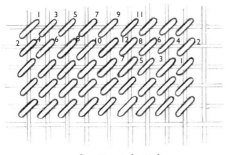

Continental stitch

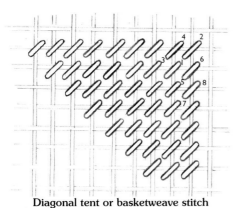

Diagonal tent or basketweave stitch

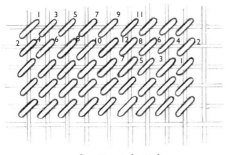

Half-cross stitch

Hint: The continental stitch is usually worked in horizontal rows, which distorts the canvas. When you're covering backgrounds and large stitching areas, use the diagonal tent stitch or basketweave; it doesn't distort the canvas as much as the continental.

Diagonal tent stitches lie better on the canvas and give a more even look if the diagonal rows flow with the grain of the mono canvas. Look carefully at the intersections of the canvas—half the time the vertical thread is on top of the intersection and half the time the horizontal thread is on top of the intersection.

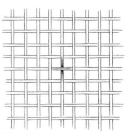

Mono canvas intersection with horizontal thread on top

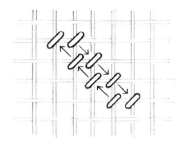

Stitching down the vertical and up the horizontal

Hint: To stitch with the grain, locate an intersection where the vertical thread is on top of the intersection. Stitch down a diagonal row by stitching only on the intersections where the vertical thread is on top. Stitch back up the return row over the intersections where all horizontal threads are on top.

Hint: Slide down the vertical threads and walk up the horizontal threads.

UP AND DOWN AND TENT STITCH

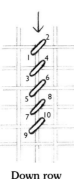

Tent stitches may be used to stitch single lines or outline an area. Make all stitches away from the body when you're stitching down a single row.

Make all stitches toward the body when you're stitching up a row.

Down row

Up row

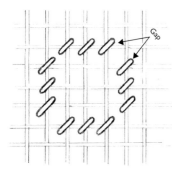

Gap around a curve

When you're stitching around a curve there are gaps in the stitches. This is perfectly okay; the eye automatically fills in the gaps.

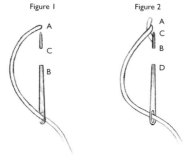

Figure 1   Figure 2

Outline stitch

To achieve a very smooth curve, use the outline or stem stitch or couch the line.

How to Couch an Outline

There are two threads involved in couching: a larger thread that stays on top of the ground fabric and actually makes the outline and a thinner thread to attach the thicker thread to the fabric. Couching is appropriate for every form of embroidery and is the main technique used in gold work.

1. Thread a needle with the thicker thread and place a waste knot on top of the ground fabric in the path the couching will go. (In the case of gold work, see page 63 for starting and stopping the threads.)

2. Bring the thread to the top.

3. Thread one strand of floss or couching thread in a small couching needle (size 9 or 10 crewel needle). For canvas: Place a tiny knot in the end of the thread, cut off any excess thread beyond the knot, and place the knot on the back of the canvas. If you're working in a blank canvas area, pierce a canvas thread when you bring the needle up. If you're working in an area where there is stitched work, make a pinhead stitch (see page 54). For fabric: place the knot on back of the fabric, bring the needle to the top, and make a pinhead stitch in the area to be couched. Place the thicker thread on the outline on the top of the ground fabric. Leave the thicker end on top of the work to be dealt with at a later time.

4. Bring the couching needle up next to the thicker thread and down on the other side of the thicker thread so the couching thread straddles the thicker thread. Couching stitches should be perpendicular to the thicker thread.

5. Place the couching stitches at even intervals, about every ¼ of an inch. When you're couching around a tight corner, place the couching stitches closer together to make the curve.

6. Once the thicker thread has been attached, take the couching thread to the back of the work and park it. Sink the thicker thread to the back with a sinking needle (see page 63).

7. Whip the thicker thread to the back of the work with the couching thread. Put a loop through the couching thread and cut off.

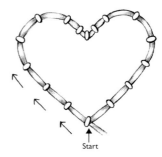

Start

Couching a heart motif

Hint: On canvas, maintaining even intervals can be a challenge. To maintain the intervals, split a canvas thread.

COUCHING TIPS

- Always couch in a clockwise direction.

- Couch tautly.

- Couch an outline last, after all the stitched areas are completed.

- When you're couching a curve between two completed stitched areas, do not couch to the finished stitches; couch to make the curve perfect regardless of whether it covers the stitches completely or not.

- Maintain a consistent over-twist on the thread being couched.

- Always place couching stitches at equal intervals.

- Couching stitches are always perpendicular to the thread being couched.

- Japanese gold is traditionally couched in a pair of threads.

- When making couching stitches, bring the needle straight up next to the thicker thread, and take the needle straight down next to the thicker thread. This makes the couching stitch the exact width of the thicker thread. Too small a stitch pinches the thicker thread; too large a stitch does not secure the thicker thread.

Stitch Diagrams

Following are some of the most often used stitches for needlepoint and embroidery, grouped according to where they work best: small areas, areas that need to be raised, narrow lines and outlines, and large areas. But do experiment—the mosaic stitch, for example, may be perfect in a large area.

> **Hint:** Experiment with one stitch using several different types of threads.

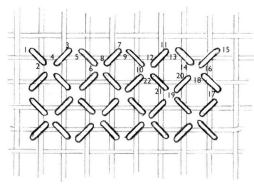

Alternating continental stitch

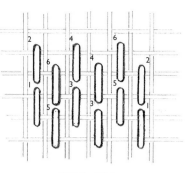

Brick stitch

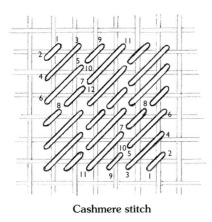

Cashmere stitch

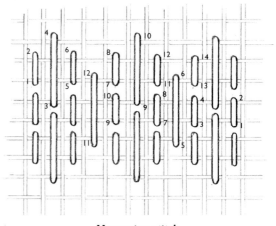

Hungarian stitch

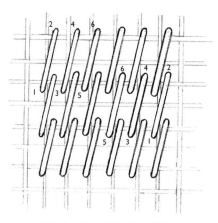

Interlocking Gobelin stitch

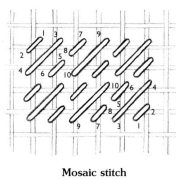

Mosaic stitch

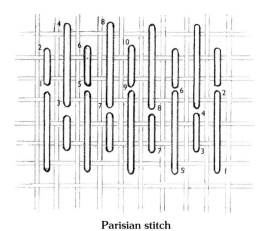

Parisian stitch

Upright Gobelin or satin stitch

TEXTURED STITCHES FOR AREAS THAT NEED TO BE RAISED

(Trees, Shrubs, Clothing, and Ground Cover)

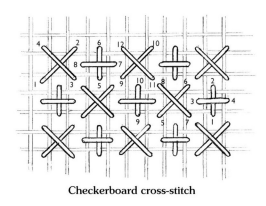

Checkerboard cross-stitch

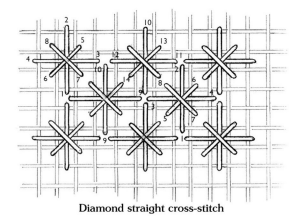

Diamond straight cross-stitch

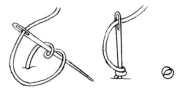

French knot

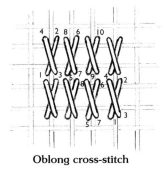

Oblong cross-stitch

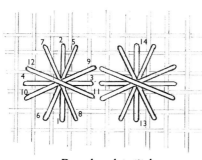

Round eyelet stitch

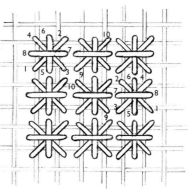

Smyrna cross-stitch

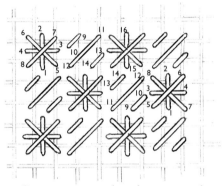

Smyrna cross-stitch and mosaic stitch combination

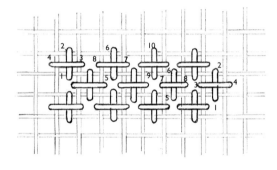

Upright cross-stitch

STITCHES FOR STEMS OR NARROW LINES AND OUTLINING

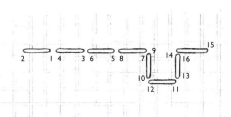

Back stitch

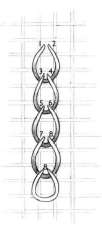

Chain stitch

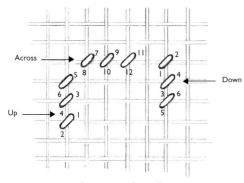

Continental stitch

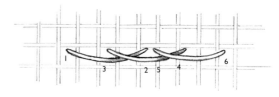

Outline stitch

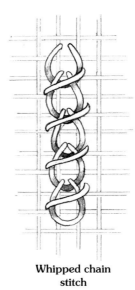

**Whipped chain
stitch**

STITCHES FOR BACKGROUNDS AND LARGE AREAS

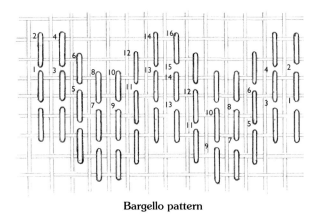

Bargello pattern

Couching in brick pattern

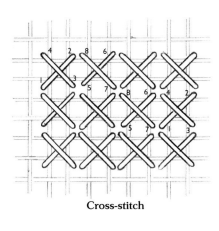

Cross-stitch

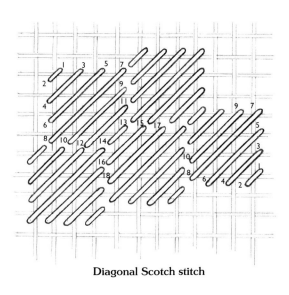

Diagonal Scotch stitch

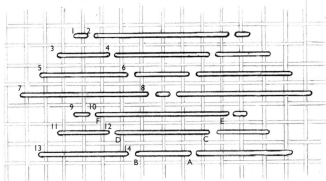

Horizontal Milanese stitch

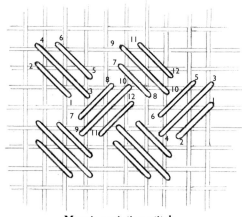

Mosaic variation stitch

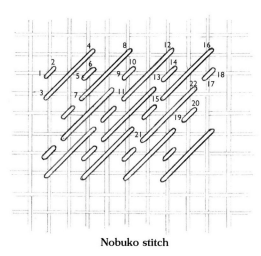

Nobuko stitch

Plaited Gobelin stitch

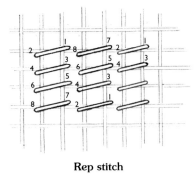

Rep stitch

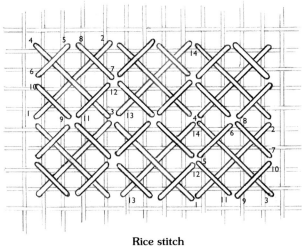

Rice stitch

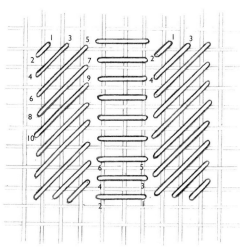

Slanted Gobelin stitch and straight Gobelin stitch combined

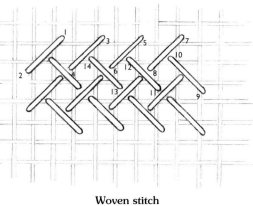

Woven stitch

MISCELLANEOUS STITCHES

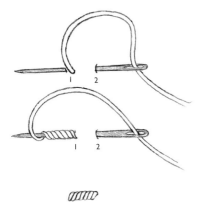

Bullion knot

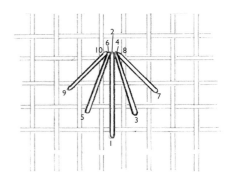

Diamond Ray stitch

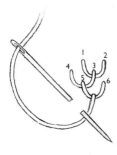

Feather stitch

Fly stitch

FINDING THE RIGHT STITCH

There are hundreds of stitches from which to choose. The stitch diagrams on the previous pages are just a sampling. Here are some additional tips:

- Think about the piece before you begin stitching; identify the various elements—small areas, large areas, areas that need texture, and so on—of the design.

- Keep a notebook with diagrams and threads that worked well in certain areas on previous projects.

- There are many stitch diagram books on the market; they are wonderful reference tools. When choosing a book, select the one with diagrams that are easiest for you to follow.

- When working with a stitch new to you, practice it before starting the actual project. Be sure to work with the same fabric and thread.

- Experiment—the only limits are one's imagination.

Compensating the Stitches

A decorative stitch can fit just perfectly into a uniform area, but in irregular-shaped areas the stitch needs to be made to accommodate the irregular shape. Portions of the stitch will often need to be shortened or lengthened. This technique is called compensating the stitch.

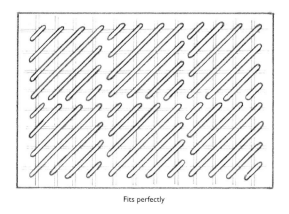

Fits perfectly

Scotch stitch in a square

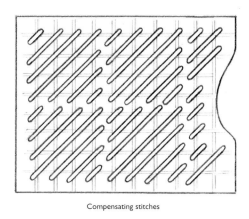

Compensating stitches

Series of Scotch stitches in an irregular area

COMPENSATING TIPS

- Start stitching in the center of the irregular pattern to get the stitch going properly and to get comfortable with the repeat pattern.

- Stitch the full stitches completely and then go back and compensate around the edges.

- It is very hard to start a return row with compensating stitches. Skip to where a full repeat of the stitch can be made and stitch the return row from that point on.

- If you have trouble visualizing how to compensate, make a complete stitch and notice where it crosses the design line. Take the stitch back out and adjust the stitch length to conform to the design line.

- In general, stitch patterns are shortened to compensate. There are instances, however, when a stitch would be lengthened. An example: One single fabric thread needs to be covered. In this case, lengthen the stitch to cover that single fabric thread.

FIXING MISTAKES

- If you place the *needle in the wrong hole or space*, take the needle off the thread and use the laying tool (see page 40) to lift the thread out of the hole. This causes the least damage to the thread. Rethread the needle and proceed.

- If you have to *remove an entire row* of stitching, take the needle off the thread and, with the laying tool, pull the thread out of each hole or space. Finish off the thread and discard it.

- If the *repeat on a decorative stitch* is not quite the same as the stitch diagram, just keep repeating the same mistake and consider it a new pattern.

- If you do not *like an area* of stitches for any reason—bad tension, the color chosen, the thread used, or the stitch just looks odd—cut the stitch or stitches out. Slip the sharp point of the scissors under each individual stitch, raising the stitch up with the point before cutting the thread. Check before cutting that the thread is free of the ground fabric.

- If you *cut a single canvas or linen thread*, keep stitching as if it did not happen.

- If you *cut a couple of canvas or linen threads*, put a small piece of clear cellophane tape on the front and back of the cut threads. Thread a sharp needle and make stitches right through the tape.

• If you cut *a large opening* in the canvas or linen, it will require reweaving. From the extra fabric around the edges, carefully clip out longer but the same number of threads as the number cut. Replace warp threads with warp threads and weft threads with weft threads by weaving the new threads into the fabric vertically and/or horizontally beyond the cut area on all sides. Follow the over and under of the weave of the fabric. Stitch over the rewoven portion.

Hint: Another method to fix a large opening in canvas: Cut out a square of canvas that is a little larger than the area to be mended. Baste the square to the back of the canvas, matching the holes of each piece perfectly. Stitch through the holes as if they were one piece of canvas.

BLOCKING, FRAMING, AND FINISHING

Blocking Needlepoint

Even work stitched on a roller frame, strecher strips, or worked in hand may become distorted. If the corners are not square and/or if the edges ripple, the piece needs to be blocked.

How to Block

1. Cover the board with the brown paper so that none of the color on the board will come off on the work.

2. Place the piece on the board. If the piece has raised stitches, place it stitched side up; if the stitches are flat, place it stitched side down. Staple it to the board in the middle of one side of the excess canvas.

Materials
Blocking board—particle board, ceiling tile
Heavy brown paper
Staple gun and stainless steel staples
T-square

Hint: If the dry work does not give enough to conform to the straight edges of the T-square, lightly spray the work with distilled water. Don't wet the canvas; just dampen it enough to loosen the starch at the intersections so the intersections move. Before spraying, test the canvas and all threads for colorfastness. If the canvas or threads are labeled Dry Clean Only, do not spray the canvas; try to pull it into shape. Very out-of-shape pieces may be dunked quickly in water before blocking. Before submerging, test the canvas and all threads for colorfastness. Block immediately.

3. Place the T-square on one edge of the canvas and staple the canvas straight along the T-square. Place staples every ⅛ of an inch.

4. Turn the corner and staple the second side straight along the T-square.

5. Block all four sides in this manner (on the fourth side, you may have to pull strenuously to align the edge with the T-square).

6. Leave the work on the board for at least 24 hours. If necessary, repeat the process. The board must remain flat throughout the blocking process and away from any source of heat.

Framing

Take the piece to a reliable framer and ask to have it museum mounted. Specifying museum mounting means that all the mounting and mat boards will be acid free (acid can cause discoloration and, in some cases, holes in the work). Old conventional wisdom dictated that needlework be framed without being covered. Now the wisdom is that the work should be covered with either glass or acrylic with spacers between the glass and finished work. This allows the stitching to breathe.

Hint: While glass is fine, a museum-quality piece of acrylic, which will screen out a very high percentage of the ultraviolet rays that cause damage to needlework, is the best choice. The drawbacks to acrylic are that it costs more than glass and it scratches easily, so be careful in the packing or dusting process.

Hint: To decide whether a piece needs a mat, try a variety of mat corners at the framer. Does the piece look better with or without a mat? About 95% of the time, mats serve to move the frame away from the finished piece so the viewer can concentrate on the piece. Keep the mat and frame at a minimum; the work should be the first thing a viewer sees. The frame should just stop the viewer's eyes from trailing off the work.

Old conventional wisdom dictated that a piece should be laced to a backing prior to framing. The new thinking is not to lace. Lacing causes weakness in the ground fabric where the lacing threads penetrate, and it can make a line run across the finished work following the lacing holes. To attach a piece to backing in lieu of lacing, use double-sided, acid-free tape, stainless steel staples, or stitch the piece to linen with a running stitch and then lace the linen.

Finishing

If you aren't comfortable with the ins and outs of finishing (which may require upholstery skills, for one), take finished pillows, chair seats, and bell pulls to your local needlework store. Almost all stores have finishing departments to do the work.

CLEANING NEEDLEWORK

All cleaning must be approached with extreme care.

- Send the piece to a very reliable dry cleaner and ask to have it cleaned only. Do not have it pressed; the large steam pressers can damage the threads and/or cause some colors to run.

- If all threads and fabrics have been tested for colorfastness and all color is true, wash the piece with a very mild commercial dishwashing liquid with no additives or scents or a specialty cleaning product available at needlework stores. Add a small amount of cleaning product to cold water and place the piece flat in the water; do not agitate, just let it soak for about ten minutes. Remove and rinse the piece until the rinse water is clean enough for you to drink (soap residue is harmful to needlework). Do not wring dry. Place the piece flat on a bath towel, face down, and press with a dry iron. Never use steam; the iron can spit particles with the steam and soil the piece.

- To remove dirt and dust from a piece that cannot be cleaned in the first two ways: Hang the piece from a line with clothespins (cushion the places that the clothespins touch the original with pieces of soft cloth). With a hair dryer set on low, blow air from the front and back and side to side. While this method will not remove spots, it will remove dust and dirt.

RESOURCES

The American Needlepoint Guild (ANG)

PO Box 1027

Cordova, TN 38088

(901) 755-3728; e-mail anginfo@needlepoint.org; website www.needlepoint.org

ANG is a national, nonprofit membership organization dedicated to needlepoint with chapters across the country. Membership in a chapter or at large is open to all. A few of the programs offered are: seminars, cyberworkshops, correspondence courses, judging certification, and a bimonthly membership magazine.

The Embroiderers' Guild of America (EGA)

335 W Broadway, Suite 100

Louisville, KY 40202

(502) 589-6956; e-mail egahq@aol.com; website www.egausa.org

EGA is a national, nonprofit membership organization focusing on a wide range of needle arts with chapters across the country. Membership, either in a local guild or at large, is open to all. Programs offered include seminars, correspondence courses, exhibitions, and a quarterly membership magazine.

The National Needlework Association (TNNA)

1100-H Brandywine Blvd.

Zanesville, OH 43702

(740) 455-6773; e-mail tnna.info@offinger.com; website www.tnna.org

TNNA is an industry trade organization comprised of manufacturers, wholesalers, distributors, publishers, and retailers of needlework supplies. The organization holds four trade shows per year for needlework retailers to buy products, and it maintains general information about the needlework industry, including material on opening and running a needlework store. Individuals may access the website for a listing of independent retailers in their area.

Abrasions 23, 24
Aida fabric 14
alternating continental stitch 59, 80
American Needlepoint Guild 108
away waste knot 55
Back stitch 88
bargello 8
bargello pattern 91
basketweave stitch 54, 60, 69–72
bead embroidery 9
blackwork 7, 55, 57
blocking 104–105
Blue Line, see waste canvas
braids 25
brick stitch 59, 80
bullion knot 97
Canvas 10–13, 15, 19, 21, 23, 24, 26, 27, 30, 71, 72, 77
canvas work, see needlepoint
canvaswork silk 24
cashmere stitch 59, 81
chain stitch 88
checkerboard cross-stitch 84
chenille needle(s) 33, 35, 63

Chinese embroidery 24
cleaning 107
clipper scissors 39
color 6, 19, 20, 28, 31–32
colorfastness 32
compensating 100–101
congress cloth 13
continental stitch 14, 54, 59, 69–72, 89
cotton fabric 10, 13, 14, 24
cotton thread(s) 17, 18, 20, 29
cotton/rayon fabric 15
couching 27, 57, 75, 76–78
couching in brick pattern 91
couching needle(s) 35
couching thread 58, 65
count(s) 10–15, 19, 28, 29, 30
counted ground, see fabric(s)
counted thread 6, 7, 8, 10, 13, 14
crewel needle(s) 33, 37, 62
crewel wool 9, 19, 28
crewelwork 9,15, 19
cross-stitch 6, 13, 14, 24, 33, 68, 92
Darners 33, 37

deluxe canvas 10
denier 10
design size 45
diagonal Scotch stitch 92
diagonal stitch(es) 27
diagonal tent stitch 54, 60, 69–72, 73
diamond ray stitch 97
diamond straight cross-stitch 84
dimensional work, see stumpwork
direction of stitching 15
double mesh canvas 12
double running stitch 7
drawn thread work 8
dual fabric(s) 6, 13, 71
dual threads 12
duo canvas 12
dye lot(s) 19, 32
Embossed work, see stumpwork
Embroiderers' Guild of America 108
embroidery hoops 50–52
embroidery needle(s) 33, 37
embroidery scissors 39
embroidery, bead 9
embroidery, pulled thread 8

embroidery, ribbon 9
embroidery, surface 6, 10, 15, 24
ending a thread 59–62
evenweave 6, 8, 9, 10, 12, 13, 14, 15
Fabric(s) 6–16, 17, 19, 24, 25, 26, 27, 30, 45
fabric count, see count
fabric, care 16
fabric, preparing 14
fabric, storage 16
feather stitch 98
finishing 106
flame stitch, see bargello
flat silk 24
Florentine embroidery, see bargello
floss, see also cotton thread(s) 17, 20, 21, 28, 29
floss silk 24
fly stitch 98
four-sided stitch 7
framing 105–106
French knot 85
Gauge, see count(s)
gold work 76
grain 15

ground, see fabric(s)
Half-cross stitch 9, 69–72
½-thread method 57
handpainted canvas 30
Hardanger 9
holding the needle 35–36
hoops, see embroidery
    hoops
horizontal Milanese stitch 93
hue 31
Hungarian point, see
    bargello
Hungarian stitch 59, 81
Interlocking canvas 12
interlocking Gobelin stitch
    59, 82
intersection(s) 11, 12, 27,
    73
Japanese embroidery 24
Kinking 22
kloster block(s) 9
knot on the back 57
L stitch 56, 62
lacing 48, 106
lamps 40
laying tool 23, 26, 40–41
lights 40
linen fabric 8, 10, 15, 19,
    24

linen thread(s) 24
linen twill, see crewelwork
long-and-short combinations
    23
Magnets 36
metal threads 25, 62
metallic braid(s) 25
metallic ribbon(s) 25
metallic thread(s) 25–26, 62
milliners needles 33
mistakes 102–103
mono canvas 11, 12, 71,
    73
mosaic stitch 59, 82
mosaic variation stitch 93
mounting fabric 45–52
National Needlework Associ-
    ation, The 109
needle(s) 20, 22, 23, 33–37
needle threader 38, 67
needle, sinking 63–65
needle, threading 66–67
needlepoint 6, 7, 13, 20,
    21, 24, 28, 33, 68, 71
needle-weaving 8, 9
Nobuko stitch 94
nonevenweave fabric(s) 10,
    15
nonstitchable threads 17,

25, 27, 63
nonstranded 19, 24, 26
novelty thread(s) 25
Oblong cross-stitch 85
outline stitch 75, 89
overdyed thread(s) 21, 32
over-twist 22
Padded work, see stump-
    work
Parisian stitch 59, 83
pearl cotton, see Perle
    Cotton
Penelope canvas, see duo
    canvas
Perle Cotton 20–22
Persian yarn 17, 19, 28
pinhead stitch(es) 9, 54–55,
    57, 58, 61
plaited Gobelin stitch 94
plastic canvas 13
ply 17
pulled thread embroidery 8,
    55
Raised work, see stumpwork
raveling 26
rayon thread(s) 26, 56, 62
reeled silk 24
rep stitch 95
ribbon embroidery 9, 35

ribbons 25, 26, 62
rice stitch 95
roller frame 45–48
round eyelet stitch 86
S-twist 22
satin stitch 9, 83
scissors 39
Scotch stitch 100
seed beads 9
selvedge 11, 12, 15
separating strands, see
    stripping
sharps needles 33
silk and wool 19
silk fabric 10, 24
silk gauze 14
silk thread(s) 17, 23–24, 30
single-weave fabric(s) 6
sinking needle 63–65
six-stranded cotton 20, 29,
    58
slanted Gobelin and straight
    Gobelin stitch combina-
    tion 96
Smyrna cross-stitch 86
Smyrna cross-stitch and
    mosaic stitch combina-
    tion 87
spun silk 24

stab method 52
starting a thread 53–58
starting a couching thread 58
starting to stitch 66–67
stem stitch 75
stitch diagrams 79–98
stitchable threads 17–26
stitch in hand 45
stitching with metallic threads 26
stitching with Perle Cotton 21
stitching with silk 23
stitching with wool threads 20
strand(s) 17, 18, 21, 23, 24, 26, 28 30, 33
stretcher bars 49
stripping threads 18, 23, 26
stumpwork 8
surface embroidery 6, 10, 15, 24, 35
synthetic thread(s) 17
Tapestry needle(s) 33–34
tapestry yarn 19
tension 20, 22
tent stitch 9, 68–74

texture(s) 25
thread(s) 17–32
thread coverage 27–30
thread length 26, 66
thread, ending, see ending a thread
thread, starting, see starting a thread
threading the needle 66
transferring a design 43–44
twill, see crewelwork
twist 22
Uncounted ground 9, 13
upright cross-stitch 87
upright Gobelin stitch 59, 83
upright stitch(es) 8, 27, 55
Value 31, 32
value scale 31
variegated thread(s) 32
Warp 11, 12, 14, 15
waste canvas 13
waste ending 60
waste knot 53–54
weaving in 59–60
weft 11, 12, 15
whipped chain stitch 90
whipping down threads 62

whitework, also see pulled thread and Hardanger 57
wool fabric 10, 14
wool thread(s) 17, 19–20, 25, 28
woven stitch 96
Z-twist   22

INDEX TO CHARTS

Appropriate tapestry needle sizes 34
Crewel wool coverage 28
Persian wool coverage 28
Silk thread coverage 30
Six-stranded cotton (floss) coverage 29
Stitching with Perle Cotton 21
Thread length 66

INDEX TO TIPS

Buying in dye lots 19
Caring for needles 37
Changing colors 31
Choosing the right stitch 67
Compensating tips 101
Couching tips 78
Determining and maintaining twist 22
Direction of stitching on canvas 15
Finding the right stitch 99
How to determine if the needle is the right size 34
How waste canvas works 13
Laying tool hints 42
Laying tools—what could be wrong 42
Park your needle 36
Pinhead stitches 61
Preparing the fabric 14
Stab method 52
Stitching with metallic threads 26
Stitching with silk 23
Stripping stranded threads 18
Techniques for stitching with wool threads 20
Up and down and tent stitch 74
Using a laying tool 41